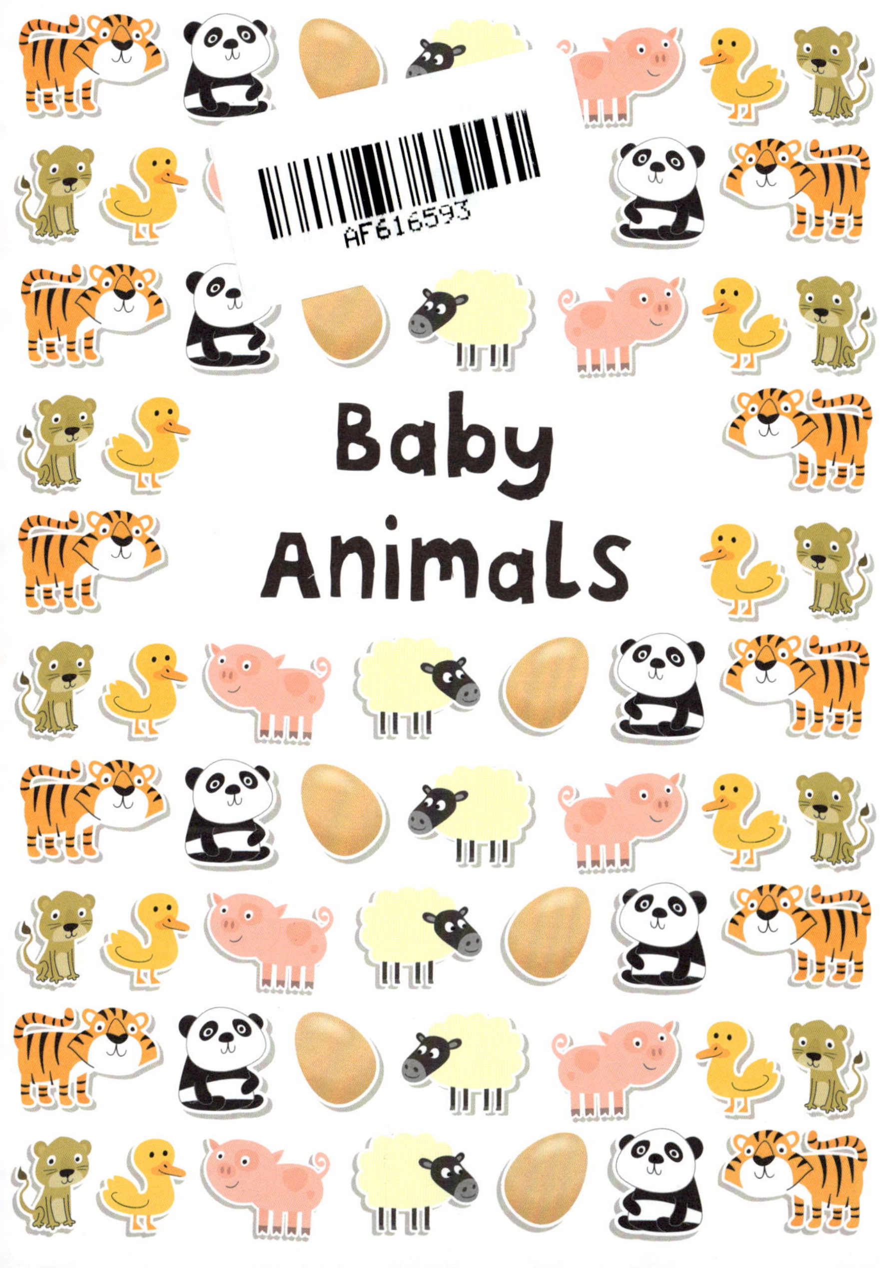
AF616593
Baby
Animals

At the nursery

The chicks are hatching. Can you find more egg stickers for the nursery?

Felicity the foal

Trace over the dotted line to draw Felicity, then colour her in.

Pet shop

Can you find and circle five differences between the two pictures?

Missing tails

All of their tails are missing!
Can you find the stickers?

Matching the cubs

Find the stickers then trace the lines to join the matching cubs.

Barnyard babies

Colour in this barnyard picture.
Then add stickers of the baby animals.

Bears' picnic

Find the stickers to give the bear cubs a treat.

Kitty is lost

Can you help her back to mummy for a cuddle?

Finger puppets

Ask a grown-up to cut us out.

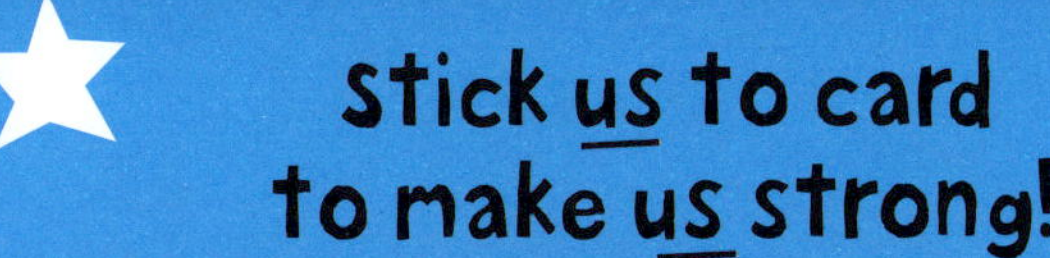

stick <u>us</u> to card
to make <u>us</u> strong!

finish the other activities first!

Sleeping bunnies

Can you circle the only bouncing bunny with your crayon?

Aliens and Monsters

Missing stars

Can you find the star stickers so the aliens can follow them home?

Home

Monster maze

Help the little monster find his way
back to the cave.

Terrible trace

Can you trace the picture of Vinny the vampire?

Now colour him in!

Alien planet

Find the alien
stickers that live on the planet.

Dot-to-dot rocket

Join the dots to finish this rocket picture.

Monster match

Trace the lines and find the matching monster stickers.

Flying Saucers
Can you find and circle five differences
between the two alien spaceships?

Finger puppets

Ask a grown-up to cut us out.

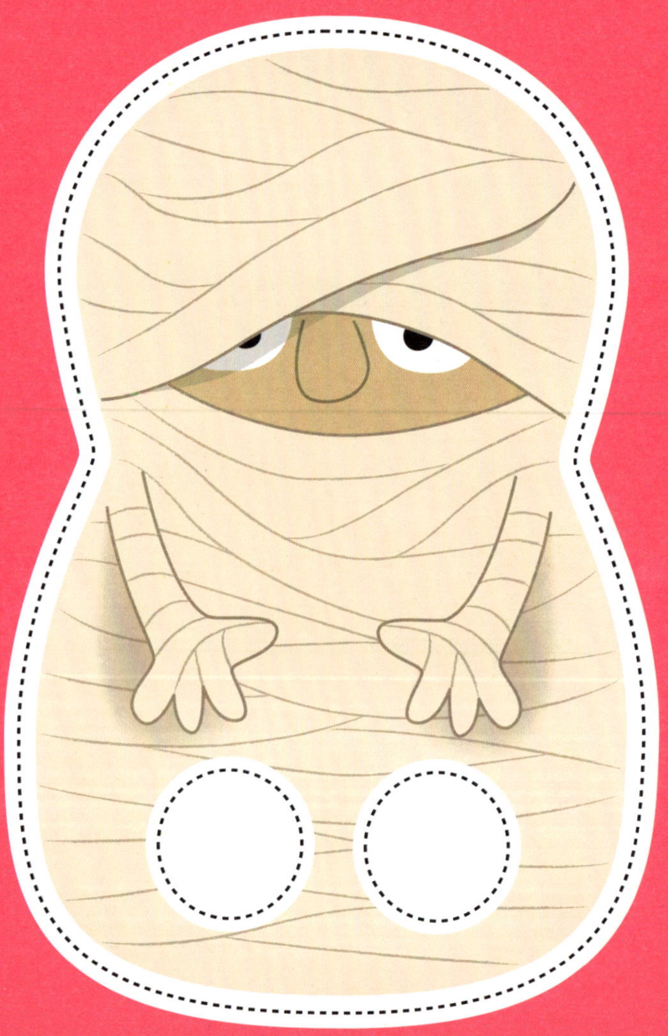

stick us to card
to make us strong!

finish the other activities first!

Monster zoo

How many monsters can you count?
Now colour in the scene.

Where is the three-eyed monster?

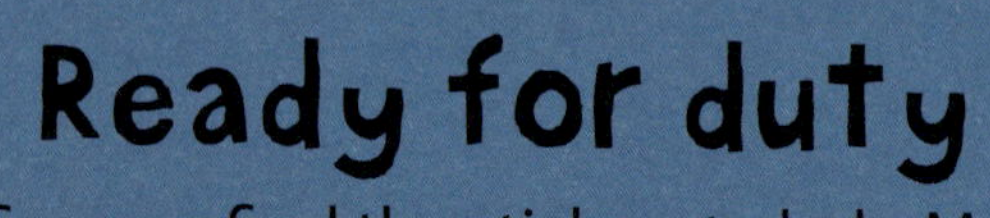

Ready for duty

Can you find the stickers to help Max the spaceman get ready for his moonwalk?

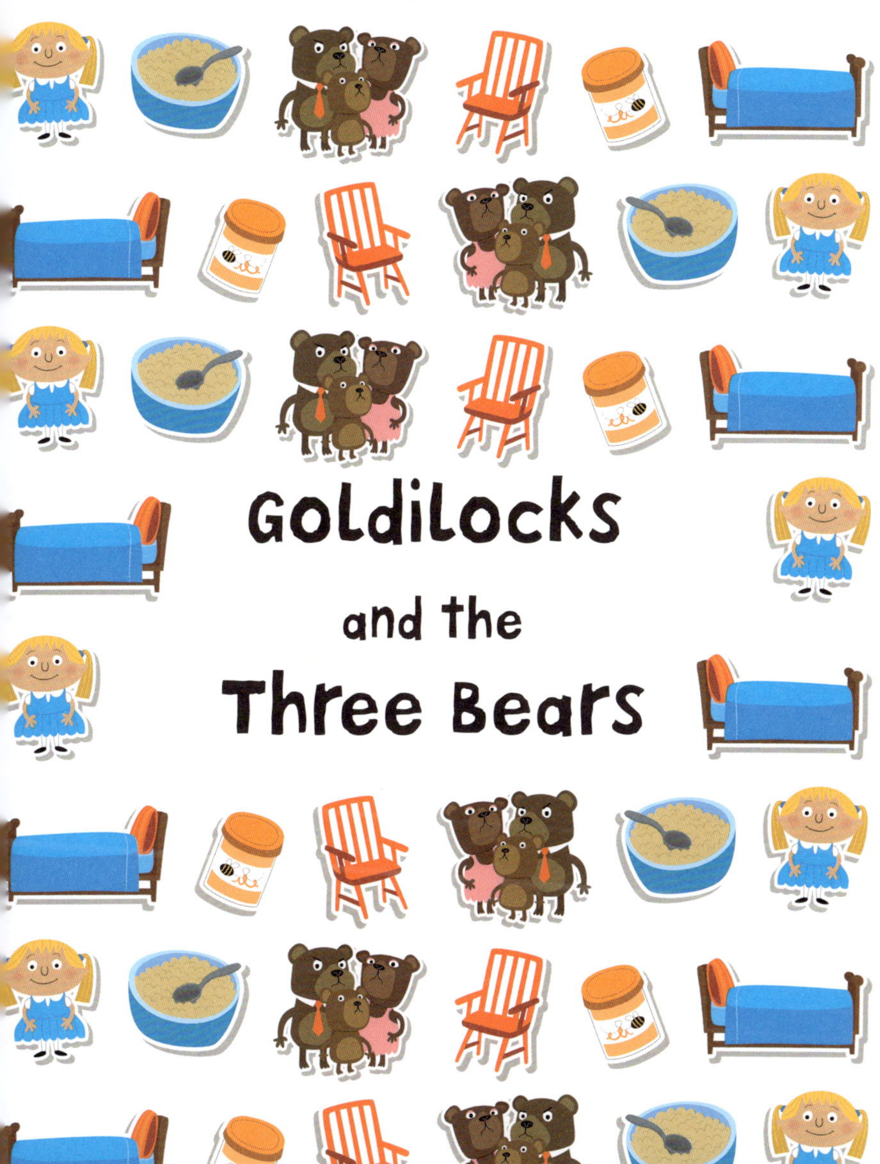

Goldilocks and the Three Bears

Goldilocks and the Three Bears

Once upon a time there was a girl called Goldilocks with golden hair, who went for a walk in the forest. She got very lost and came across a cottage, so knocked on the door. As there was no answer Goldilocks went in.

Goldilocks was very hungry. On the table were three bowls of steaming hot porridge. She tried the first bowl but it was too hot. The second bowl was too cold, but the third bowl was just right. She ate it all up!

After eating, Goldilocks was tired and spotted three comfy chairs. She tried the first chair but it was too high. The second chair was too low, but the third chair was just right. But as she sat, it broke under her!

Goldilocks was still tired and went to the bedroom to lie down. Inside were three beds. She tried the first bed but it was too hard. The second bed was too soft, but the third bed was just right. She climbed in and fell fast asleep!

Soon after the three bears, who lived in the cottage, came home ready to eat their porridge.

"Somebody's been eating my porridge?" growled Daddy Bear.

"Somebody's been eating my porridge?" said Mummy Bear.

"Somebody's been eating my porridge, and it's all gone!" cried Baby Bear!

The bears then went into the living room to sit down.

"Somebody's been sitting in my chair?" growled Daddy Bear.

"Somebody's been sitting in my chair?" said Mummy Bear.

"Somebody's been sitting in my chair, and they've broken it!" cried Baby Bear!

The bears then decided to check upstairs.

"Somebody's been sleeping in my bed?" growled Daddy Bear.

"Somebody's been sleeping in my bed?" said Mummy Bear.

"Somebody's been sleeping in my bed… and she's still there!" cried Baby Bear!

Goldilocks jumped out of the bed with a cry, and ran out of the house. She never troubled the three bears ever again.

Tasty porridge

Find food stickers to make
Goldilocks' porridge even more yummy!

Time for a rest

Join the dots so Goldilocks
can take a rest, then colour it in.

Finger puppets

Ask a grown-up to cut us out.

Stick us to card
to make us strong!

finish the other activities first!

The three bears' cottage

Can you find and circle five differences between the two pictures?

Daddy is angry!

Add some teeth stickers to Daddy bear.

Three hungry bears

Can you help the bears get to their porridge?

Bedtime for bears

Add mattress and pillow stickers to make the beds now Goldilocks has left.

Get dressed quick!

Time to leave Goldilocks – find her glove and boot stickers.

Dinosaurs

Dinosaur Valley

Find the dinosaur stickers
that live in the valley.

Hungry T-rex

Rex is missing his teeth.
Can you find the stickers?

Lost egg

Help mummy dinosaur find her egg.

Draw a diplodocus

Can you trace the picture of
Danny the diplodocus?

Now colour us in!

Missing skeleton

Find the bone stickers to complete the Tyrannosaurus Rex skeleton!

Dinnertime

Can you circle the cavemen with your pencil?

Jungle nursery
How many eggs can you count?
Now colour in the scene.

Where is the hatching egg?

Finger puppets

Ask a grown-up to cut us out.

stick us to card
to make us strong!

finish the other activities first!

Dinosaurs of the deep

Can you find and circle five differences between the two scenes?

Roaring doubles

Trace the lines to join the matching pairs together, then find the stickers.

Nursery Rhymes

Humpty Dumpty

Humpty Dumpty sat on a wall,
Humpty Dumpty had a great fall.
All the king's horses,
And all the king's men,
Couldn't put Humpty together again.

All the King's horses

Circle the King's horses and count how many there are.

Twinkle Twinkle Little Star

Twinkle, twinkle, little star,
How I wonder what you are.
Up above the world so high,
Like a diamond in the sky.
Twinkle, twinkle, little star,
How I wonder what you are.

Find the star sticker

Dot-to-dot star

Join the dots to make the picture of a star.

Baa, Baa, Black Sheep

Baa, baa, black sheep,
Have you any wool?
Yes sir, yes sir, three bags full.
One for the master,
One for the dame,
And one for the little boy
Who lives down the lane.

Down the lane

Find a way through to help black sheep find the bags of wool.

Hey Diddle Diddle

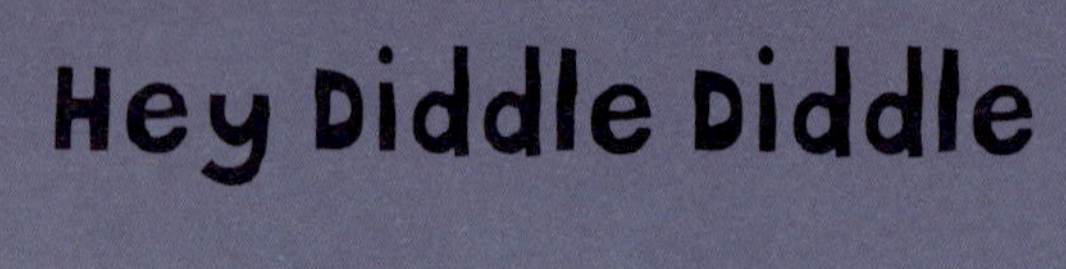

Hey diddle diddle, the cat and the fiddle,
The cow jumped over the moon.
The little dog laughed, to see such fun,
And the dish ran away with the spoon.

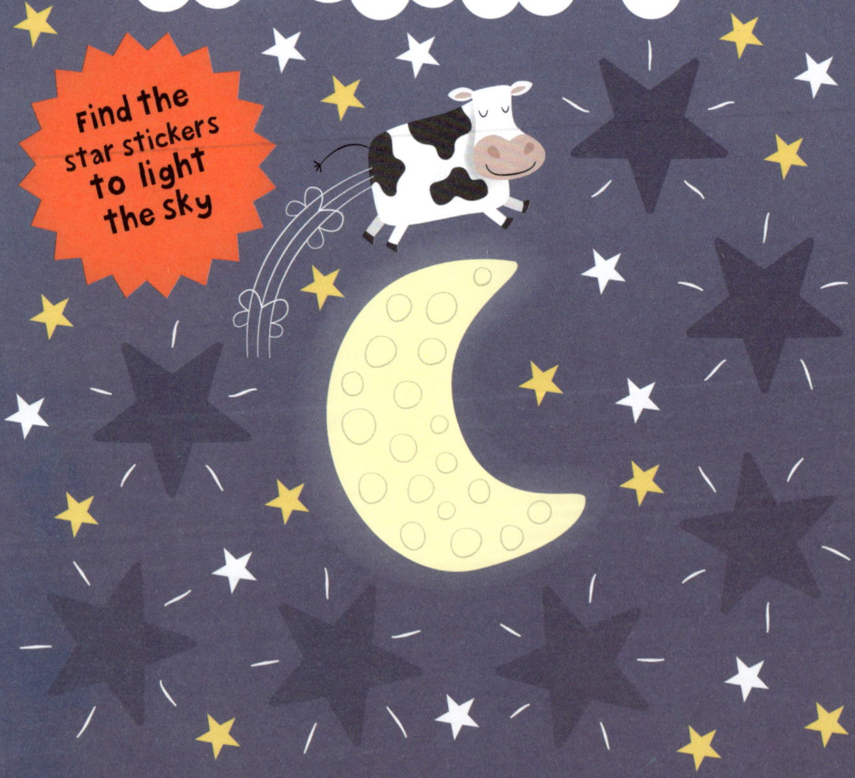

Find the star stickers to light the sky

Missing bits

Find the missing stickers to complete the picture.

Jack and Jill

Jack and Jill went up the hill
To fetch a pail of water.
Jack fell down and broke his crown,
And Jill came tumbling after.

Find the five differences between the two scenes

Little Miss Muffet

Little Miss Muffet sat on a tuffet,
Eating her curds and whey.
Along came a spider,
Who sat down beside her,
And frightened Miss Muffet away.

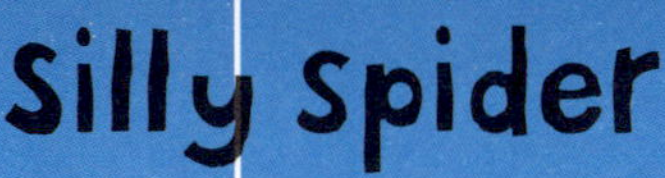

Silly Spider

Can you find the missing leg stickers?

Hickory Dickory Dock

Hickory dickory dock,
The mouse ran up the clock.
The clock struck one,
The mouse ran down,
Hickory dickory dock.

Tell the time

Can you find the missing numbers to complete the clock face?

Old Mother Hubbard

Old Mother Hubbard
Went to the cupboard,
To get her poor dog a bone.
When she got there,
The cupboard was bare,
And so the poor dog had none.

At the Zoo

Lenny the lion ROARS!

Add some more teeth stickers to Lenny's roaring mouth.

Polly the parrot

What colour should Polly be?

Now colour her in.

The penguin's pool

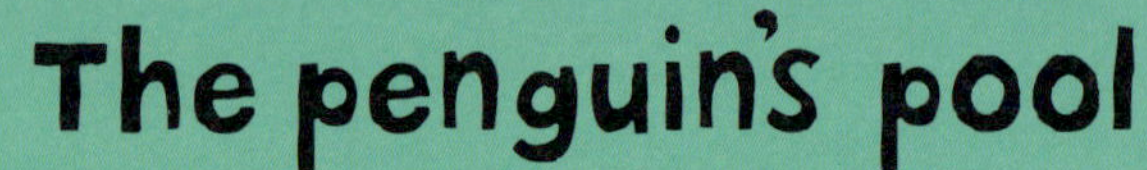

Can you find and circle five differences between the two pictures?

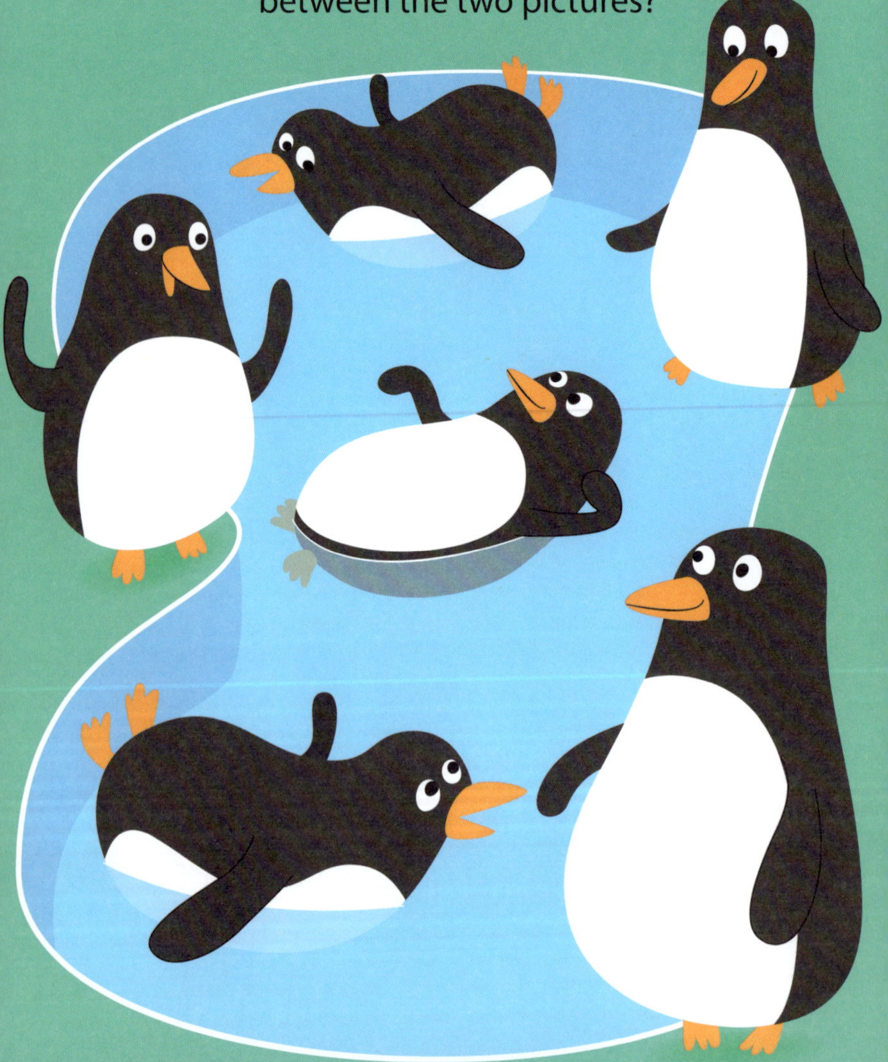

Dinnertime!

Can you find the animal stickers so the keeper can feed them?

Monkey nuts

Monkey is really hungry!
Help him find the nuts.

Reggie the rhino

Reggie has lost his horns!
Can you find the stickers?

The seals are hungry

Find the fish stickers to fill the bucket ready for dinner.

Matching friends

Can you draw the lines between the matching friends?

All things orange

Use an orange pencil or crayon to colour everything in.

Clownfish
Lobster
Tiger

Finger puppets

Ask a grown-up to cut us out.

Stick us to card
to make us strong!

finish the other activities first!

Missing stripes

Little Tiger has lost some of his stripes.
Can you help complete the drawing?

well done!

superstar!

Good job!
well done!
Winner!

superstar!

MB
DB
LB
well done!

Winner!
Good job!

superstar!

3
6
Good job!

well done!
9
12
superstar!

Winner!

well done!
superstar!

well done!

superstar!
Good job!

Good job!
superstar!

Winner!

well done!
superstar!
Good job!

Winner!
well done!

well done!

Superstar!
Winner!

superstar!
well done!

superstar!
Good job!

well done!
Winner!

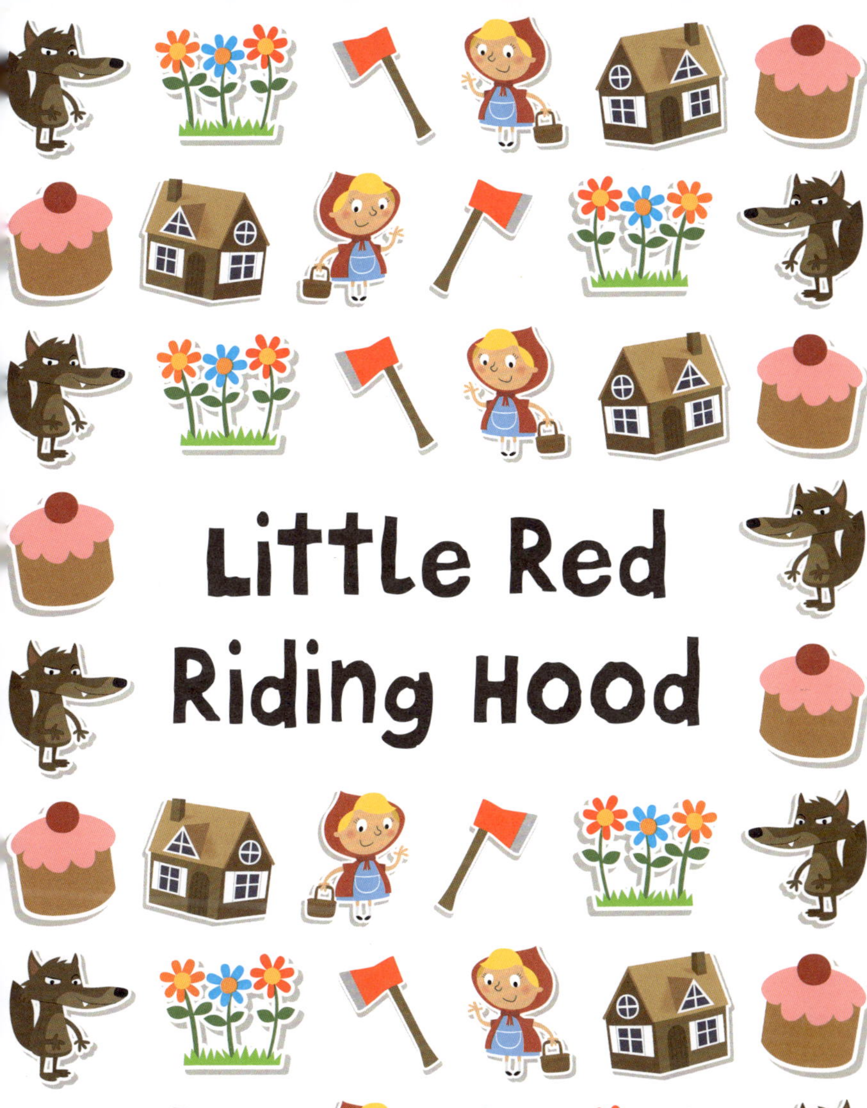

Little Red Riding Hood

Little Red Riding Hood

Once upon a time there was a little girl who wore a red cloak with a hood. Her name was Little Red Riding Hood. One day she set off to visit her grandmother on the other side of the forest. When she was leaving, her mother called after her, "Don't stop and don't talk to any strangers in the wood!"

As she wandered along the path, she thought what a beautiful day it had become. Soon after, Little Red Riding Hood bumped into Mr Wolf, who was standing by the edge of the forest path.

Forgetting what her mother had told her, she stopped and when he asked her where she was going, she replied, "To my grandmother's house." Little Red Riding Hood quickly remembered her mother's words and ran off.

It was such a lovely day and there were so many pretty flowers in the wood that Little Red Riding Hood forgot her mother's advice and stopped again – this time to pick some flowers for her grandmother.

When she arrived at her grandmother's house it was very late. Mr Wolf had run to the house and eaten her all up! Then, he put her nightdress on and hid in her bed waiting for Little Red Riding Hood.

She thought that her grandmother looked strange, but didn't know that it was Mr Wolf in disguise. "Grandmother, what big eyes you have," she said. "All the better to see you with, my dear!" said Mr Wolf, trying to sound like grandmother.

"And what big ears you have," she said. "All the better to hear you with, my dear!" replied Mr Wolf with a big smile. Little Red Riding Hood knew something was wrong.

"But what big teeth you have!" she cried out. "All the better to eat you with!" and he jumped out of bed, chasing her out of the house!

By chance, the friendly woodcutter was nearby and came to her rescue. He forced Mr Wolf to cough up scared old grandmother and then took them both home. Little Red Riding Hood promised her mother that she would never speak to strangers ever again.

Get to Grandma's

Use your pencil to help Red Riding Hood find the right path to Grandma's house.

Running Riding Hood

Trace over the dotted line to draw Red Riding Hood, then colour her in.

What's missing?

The woodcutter's axe, Red Riding Hood's basket and the wolf's tail are missing. Find the stickers.

Fill the picnic basket

Find the stickers to fill the
picnic basket with yummy treats!

Grandma's cottage
Can you find and circle five differences
between the two pictures?

Finger puppets

Ask a grown-up to cut us out.

finish the other activities first!

colouring in chase

Use your pencils and crayons to colour in the scene.

Matching pairs

Draw lines to join the matching pairs. Then find the stickers.

Best Pets

Queen of the kittens

Which kitten has a sparkling pink collar?

Goldfish bowl

Find some stickers to make this goldfish feel at home.

Vet's waiting room

Can you find and circle five differences between the two pictures?

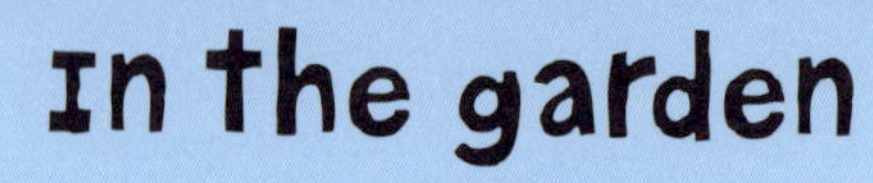

In the garden

Finish colouring in this garden scene and add some pet stickers.

Pet pals

Add the stickers and trace the lines to the matching pets.

Dot-to-dot bone

Join the dots, then decorate with bone stickers.

Bright budgie

What colour should Betty the budgie be?

Doggy dinnertime

Rex is hungry! Which trail will lead him to his food?

Playtime in the park!

Colour in the park where Rex is playing.

All things brown

Use your pencils or crayons
to colour everything in.

DOg
coconut

Dinnertime

Find the stickers to fill the cupboard with pet food.

Fairy and
Princess

Fairy garden

How many fairies can you count in the magic garden?

Now
colour
it in!

cast a spell

Join the dots to complete the picture of the wand.

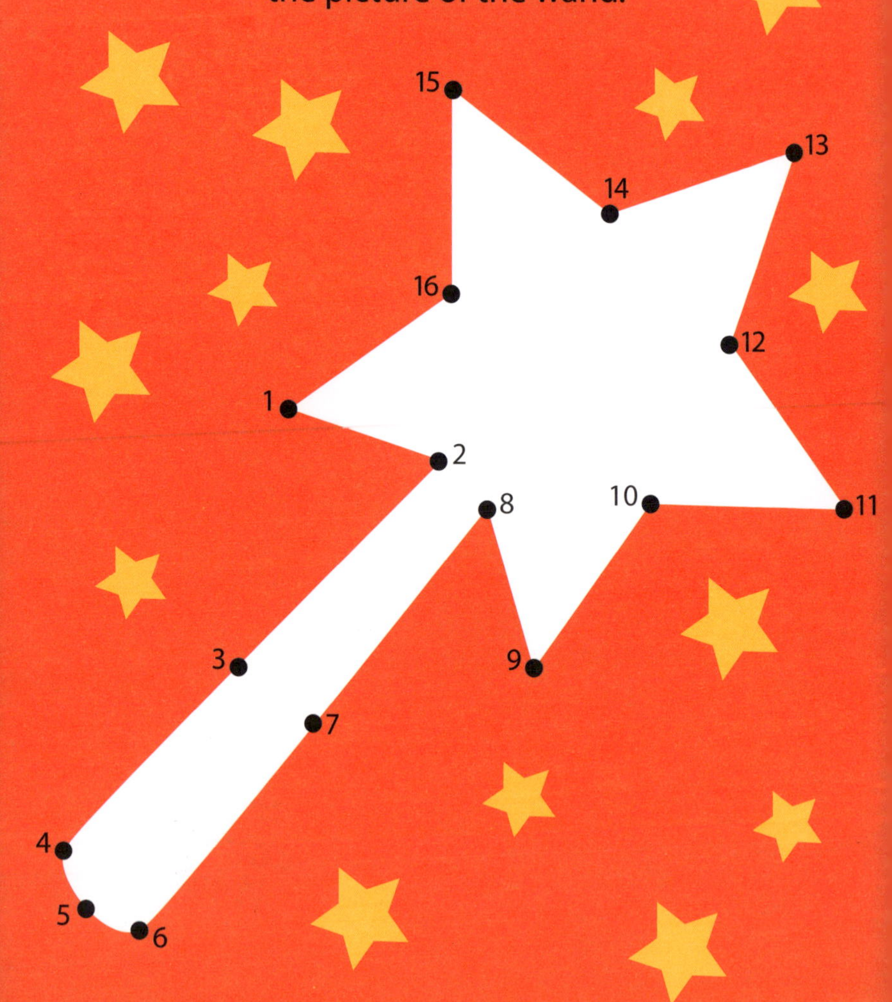

Felicity the fairy

Felicity would like some colourful wings.
Can you help?

Magic kingdom

Find the stickers to decorate the fairy world.

Princess ponies

Find the pony stickers then draw a line from the matching princess.

Royal wedding

Find the stickers to get Princess Erin ready for her wedding.

Princess Polly

Can you find the stickers
to give Polly a happy face?

Lost wand

Help Nia the fairy find her magic wand.

Finger puppets

Ask a grown-up to cut us out.

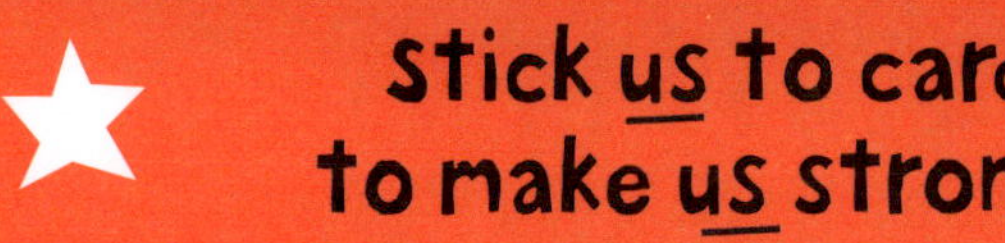

stick us to card
to make us strong!

finish the other activities first!

Fairy Princesses

Can you find and circle five differences between the two fairies?

Royal carriage

Colour in the carriage so it is ready for the ball.

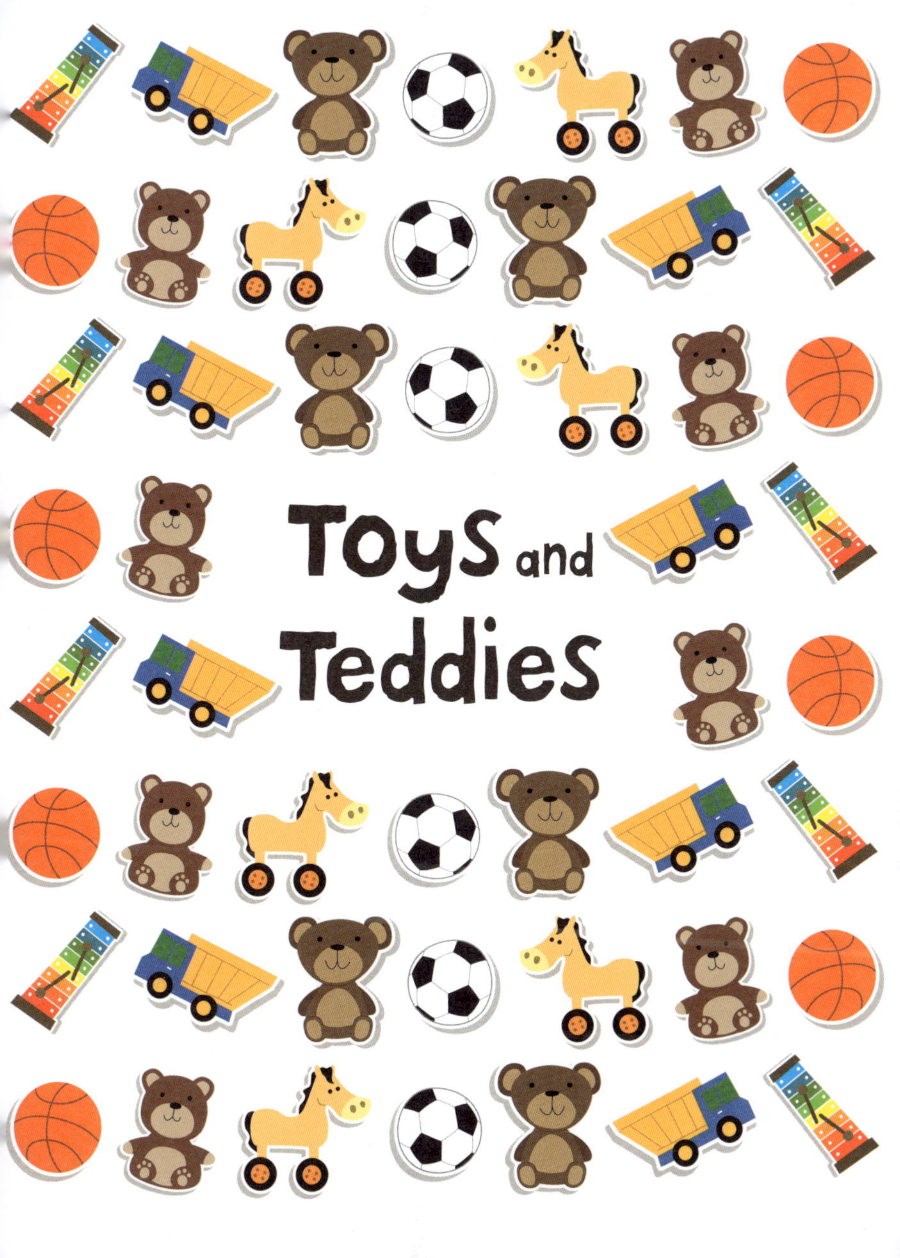
Toys and
Teddies

Playhouse

Can you colour in the playhouse?

can you spot the teddy bear?

PLAYHOUSE

Toby the teddy bear

Find the stickers to give Toby a happy face.

Jack in the box

Trace over the dotted lines to draw the jack in a box.

Now colour him in!

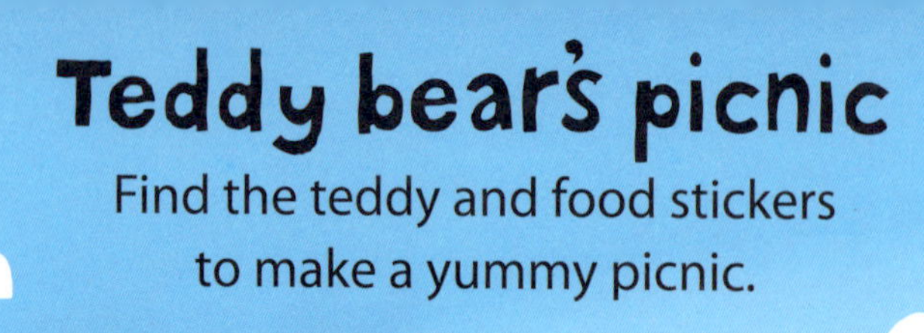

Teddy bear's picnic

Find the teddy and food stickers
to make a yummy picnic.

Messy bedroom

Find the toy stickers to make a real mess!

Choo choo dots

Join the dots and complete this picture of a toy train.

Teddy treehouse

Can you find and circle five differences between the two teddy treehouses?

Finger puppets

Ask a grown-up to cut us out.

stick us to card
to make us strong!

finish the other activities first!

Playtime on the beach

Can you count and circle the buckets?

Lost rocket

Help the toy spaceman find the right trail back to his rocket.

Game, Set and match

Find the matching stickers then trace the lines.

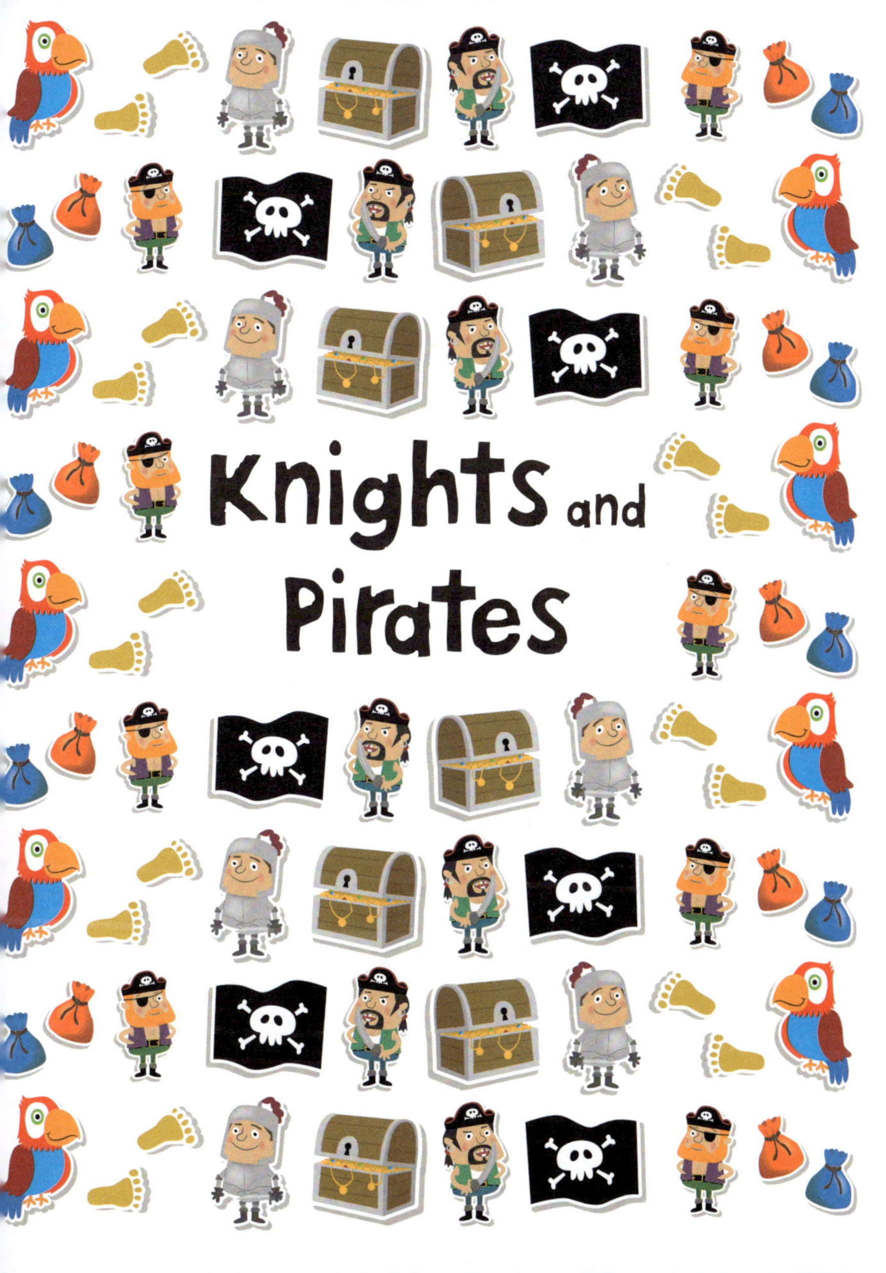
Knights and
Pirates

Pirate Ship

How many mice can you count on the boat?

Terence the brave

Find the stickers to get Terence ready for his joust.

Bright knights

How many green knights can you count?

Treasure island

Find the stickers to decorate the pirate's hideout.

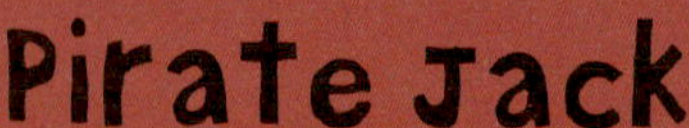

Pirate Jack

Can you find the stickers to give Jack a scary face?

Royal maze

Help Sir Laugh-a-lot follow
the maze to get to the castle!

Hero horse

Can you trace this picture of a knight's horse?

Now
colour
in both
horses!

Finger puppets

Ask a grown-up to cut us out.

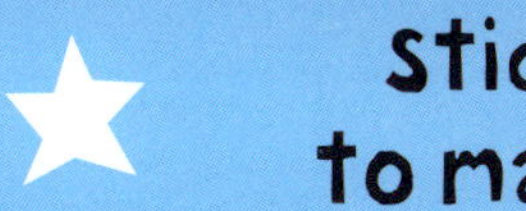

Stick <u>us</u> to card
to make <u>us</u> strong!

finish the other activities first!

Shiny Shields

Can you find and circle five differences between the two shields?

Booty bags

Find the three treasure bags, then trace the dotted lines.

The Ugly
Duckling

The Ugly Duckling

Once upon a time, there was a little duckling who was different to his brothers and sisters. He did not have yellow feathers, but grey ones. He was not small, but big. Everyone teased the ugly duckling and made him sad. His mummy tried to comfort him, but was surprised at how different he looked.

The ugly duckling was so sad that he decided to run away. He waddled along the river looking for ducklings that looked like him.

Whenever he met other birds he stopped them, "Have you seen any ducklings like me?" he asked. "What an ugly duckling," they replied, "we have never seen a duckling like you before!"

All winter he searched for other ducklings that looked like him, but he could not find any. He was very cold and very lonely.

By the time spring arrived, the ugly duckling had grown a lot. His feathers were not grey anymore, but pure white! Soon enough, he saw more birds flying through the sky. They looked exactly like him.

"Stop, stop! Who are you?" he cried. "We are swans, the same as you", they called back. "Come with us!"

The ugly duckling was so happy as he flew into the sky and followed them. He was not an ugly duckling after all, but had grown into a beautiful swan with a lovely long neck, white feathers and big strong wings.

The lonely pond
Colour in Ugly Duckling's
lonely pond scene.

Mother duck's nest

Find the egg stickers to fill the nest.

Where is duckling's beak?

Ugly Duckling is missing his beak.
Can you find the sticker?

Find new friends

Ugly Duckling has spotted some new friends.
Can you help him get to them?

Where are you?

Can you circle the swans with your crayon?

Finger puppets

Ask a grown-up to cut us out.

stick us to card
to make us strong!

finish the other activities first!

Flying family
Can you find and circle five differences between the two scenes?

Quack quack match

Trace the lines to join the matching pairs together. Then find the stickers.